Contents

Winter Survival	2
Falling Temperatures	4
Winter Preparations	6
Storing and Saving	8
Using the Sun for Warmth	10
Winter Coats	12
Snuggling for Warmth	14
Migration	16
Safety in Numbers	18
Spring Approaches	20
Index	22

WINTER SURVIVAL

Winter can be a cruel, harsh, and unforgiving season. Snow may cover the land, making both travel and the finding of food and water difficult for many animals. While freezing temperatures can rob bodies of heat essential to life, many animals have developed their own strategies for winter survival.

In summer, farmers grow hay to store and feed to stock during winter, when food is scarce.

Throughout winter, bison travel long distances to find exposed grasses.

FALLING TEMPERATURES

Temperatures begin to fall in early autumn. Deciduous trees with broad leaves respond to the shorter days and cooler nights with displays of vibrant autumn colors. The falling temperatures and the autumn frosts are first noticed by animals that live in the mountains.

In autumn, monarch butterflies "fuel up" on pollen in the Allegheny Mountains in Pennsylvania before taking off on a 3,000-mile flight to Mexico for the winter.

Ptarmigans blend into autumn foliage. Before winter comes, their plumage turns white, which helps them hide from predators.

WINTER PREPARATIONS

During the autumn months, animals that hibernate fatten up on food. Throughout the long months of winter, hibernating animals convert their body fat into energy to stay warm. Their heart rate slows down to conserve energy.

Cold-blooded salamanders survive the winter by hibernating beneath the frozen surface of ponds.

This grizzly bear is fattening up on autumn berries. In its winter den, the hibernating grizzly will convert fat into energy. It uses the energy to keep itself warm.

STORING AND SAVING

Some animals survive winter by living off stores of food that they hoarded throughout the autumn in burrows and hollow trees. During cold winter days, these animals sleep a lot and feed off of their stores, but on sunny winter days they leave their homes to hunt for extra food and sun themselves.

In the autumn, tree squirrels collect and store more nuts than they can eat. Nut caches will feed them during winter months when the trees are bare.

In Athabasca, Alaska, people dry salmon and store it for winter days when food is more difficult to find.

Using the Sun for Warmth

Both warm- and cold-blooded animals take advantage of the sun's heat on a cold winter day. Animals and birds enjoy the feel of the sun on their bodies in winter, just as we do.

This garter snake is warming itself three different ways: It absorbs radiant heat from direct sunlight and receives heat from a sun-warmed rock.

It is also conserving body heat by coiling up against itself.

An adult alligator basks in the morning sun.

WINTER COATS

Staying warm is essential to survival. Warm-blooded animals must insulate their bodies from chilly winter temperatures. Mammals have fur, which retains body heat. A fur coat traps air next to the body, just as a winter jacket traps air next to your body.

White fur blends into a snow-covered world to protect the mountain goat from predators.

A polar bear naps on frozen snow and ice. Its thick winter coat and layer of body fat provide insulation.

SNUGGLING FOR WARMTH

Snuggling is something that many species, including the human species, do to stay warm. By snuggling together, animals share each other's body warmth. They can also snuggle their unprotected noses or beaks into their bodies, in the same way we snuggle our hands up our sleeves.

MIGRATION

Seasonal migration is a special survival strategy used by many creatures. By traveling to lands with plentiful food supplies in summer and then retreating to warmer areas in winter, some species have the best of both worlds.

Polar bears make a solitary migration north to the frozen Arctic seas to hunt seals.

White pelicans are migrators. This flock is migrating north to lakes created by melting glaciers. Their large wings carry them efficiently over great distances.

SAFETY IN NUMBERS

Most migrating animals travel in flocks or herds. This gives migrators several advantages over traveling alone. One advantage is that there is some safety in big numbers against the many predators. But the best advantage might be that the younger animals can follow a leader who knows how to find the way!

When winter comes, bighorn sheep migrate to lower altitudes.

Elk travel the same migration routes to their winter ranges every year. There, away from the deep snow of the higher ranges, they find grass to graze on.

Migrating elk travel in herds to the winter range. As spring approaches, the herds will return to their mountain home.

19

SPRING APPROACHES

As the streams and lakes begin to thaw, the migrators start returning to their summer habitats. Patches of green grass begin to appear through the snow and, once again, animals can find food and water more easily. Spring is also when animals shed their winter coats. Winter is over for another year.

Grasshoppers die at the first hard autumn frost. Eggs, laid before the frosts, survive winter and hatch in spring.

As spring comes, bison gorge on the fresh, green grass.

INDEX

alligator	11
bighorn sheep	18
bison	3, 21
elk	19
garter snake	11
grasshopper	21
grizzly bear	7
humans	3, 9, 12
monarch butterfly	5
mountain goat	2, 4, 13, 20
polar bear	13, 16
ptarmigan	5, 20
salamander	6
tree squirrel	9
white pelican	17

About Buck Wilde

Observers of wildlife can often stress wild animals — especially during harsh winter months. When I was shooting the photographs for my book *Winter Survival*, I had to be careful that my presence didn't cause any animals to abandon a food source that might be vital to their survival.

The winter environment was also challenging for me as a photographer. My fingers and toes were frequently chilled by subzero temperatures. The batteries for my camera didn't last very long, and my cameras and lenses would have frozen if I hadn't handled them carefully. My film also became brittle and very hard to handle.

The advice I give to any young photographers is "take good pictures of wildlife in the warmer, friendlier months." It's easier on your subjects, your camera gear, and your fingers and toes.

WILD AND WONDERFUL
Winter Survival
Peter the Pumpkin-Eater
Because of Walter
Humphrey
Hairy Little Critters
The Story of Small Fry

ACTION AND ADVENTURE
Dinosaur Girl
Amelia Earhart
Taking to the Air
No Trouble at All!
River Runners
The Midnight Pig

FRIENDS AND FRIENDSHIP
Uncle Tease
PS I Love You, Gramps
Friendship in Action
Midnight Rescue
Nightmare
You Can Canoe!

ALL THE WORLD'S A STAGE
All the World's a Stage!
Which Way, Jack?
The Bad Luck of King Fred
Famous Animals
Puppets
The Wish Fish

Written by **Buck Wilde**
Photographed by **Buck Wilde**
Edited by **Sue Ledington**
Designed by **Amanda Gordon**
Photographic research by **Sarah Irvine**

Additional photography by **Ant Photo Library:** Dave Watts (pygmy possum hibernating, p. 6); **Hedgehog House:** John Eastcott (child, p. 12); Colin Monteath (husky sleeping, p. 14); **N.Z. Picture Library:** (p. 15); **Photobank:** (making hay, p. 3; cows, p. 14)

© 1997 Shortland Publications
All rights reserved.

05 04 03 02 01
12 11 10 9 8 7 6

Distributed in the United States of America by
Rigby
a division of Reed Elsevier Inc.
1000 Hart Road
Barrington, IL 60010-2627

Printed in Hong Kong through Colorcraft Ltd.
ISBN: 0-7901-1688-X